RETURN TO HIROSHIMA

RETURN TO HIROSHIMA

BETTY JEAN LIFTON

Photographs by Eikoh Hosoe

Atheneum   1970   New York

Mural paintings as shown on pages
12, 13, 14 and 15 by Mr. & Mrs. Iri Maruki

For Ichiro and Tokie,
who have dedicated their lives
to Hiroshima's children,
and the children of the world.

Return to Hiroshima——

    You who saw it shortly after the world's first atomic bomb had turned it into an atomic desert—August 6, 1945.

    You who watched it struggling over the years to rise out of its death-tainted ashes.

    You who have never seen Hiroshima, but to whom the name has a meaning.

Ask of the city——

    What of the old, have they forgotten?

    What of the young, do they remember?

    What of the wounded, have they healed?

On the surface Hiroshima looks like any other thriving port city in western Japan.

Ringed in by low mountains and facing the miniature islands of the Inland Sea, it exudes the charm of a small provincial town. The Ohta River still winds lazily through it, its seven fingers weaving the marshy deltas together.

Once Hiroshima was an inbred castle town, with the Emperor's troops garrisoned there. Its ships pointed toward China and the conquest of Asia. Its factories churned out munitions. Its offices bustled with prefectural affairs.

It seemed to lead a charmed life. The American B-29's that razed Tokyo, Nagoya and so many other sizeable cities, merely passed over it.

Hiroshima citizens thought that they might be spared. They were, until that morning of August 6, when they were catapulted into the nuclear age.

The castle, the shipyards, and the municipal buildings have been rebuilt. Large factories once again turn out automobiles and sewing needles. But the pride of the city is its baseball stadium, which houses the Hiroshima Carps.

Once again one goes to Hiroshima to eat the famous oysters and drink the delicious *sake,* rice wine. One wanders through the arcaded shopping areas, and relaxes in the lively entertainment quarters at night.

Only a few pilgrims, like yourself, come to look into the true face of Hiroshima.

But can this modern metropolis really be the legendary Hiroshima?

The center of the city reminds you of parts of Tokyo, or even certain cities in Europe. Once it sprawled without plan into a maze of narrow winding alleyways, but now it has been resurrected western-style with wide boulevards.

You learn that most of the population of five hundred thousand is made up of outsiders who swarmed in from other places after the war to take advantage of the frontier conditions. Many of them were destitute evacuees from Japan's overseas colonies, grateful to find a barren area where they could begin anew.

These newcomers give Hiroshima its energy. They live in the present and for the future. Should you talk to any of them, they do not seem to remember the past.

But should you talk to any of Hiroshima's ninety thousand survivors, you will find that they remember only too well. For them it is still 8:15 in the morning. The all clear has sounded. The children are on their way to school. Men and women are already at work.

A B-29 suddenly appears overhead. It is the Enola Gay, destined to share the dark immortality of the atomic bomb it now releases eighteen hundred feet over the center of the city.

There is a blinding flash of light, unbearable heat, a deafening explosion, and then a fantastic multicolored cloud rising out of itself, a poisonous mushroom growing into the sky, its fiery roots lashing out with the intensity of a tornado.

For the survivors, the Atomic Mushroom, as this cloud came to be called, still hangs over the city.

Seventy-eight thousand people are known to have been killed by the bomb. Estimates go as high as two hundred thousand or more.

Those closest to the hypocenter (above which the bomb exploded) were incinerated on the spot by the extreme heat, or perished in the flames that tore through the streets.

Many others, within a mile and a half radius of the blast, succumbed shortly afterwards from flash burns and the intense dosage of radiation.

The strength of the *pikadon*, the flash boom, as the bomb came to be called, was equivalent to twenty thousand tons of TNT. We are making bombs with a thousand times that strength today.

13

The survivors soon realized that this was no ordinary bomb.

Within hours or days after exposure, even those who were seemingly uninjured, developed strange symptoms. At first there was nausea, vomiting, diarrhea, fever, then purple spots on various parts of their bodies. Blood issued from the gums, throat, rectum and urinary tract. Their hair began to fall out, and their white blood cell count dropped. For many there was gradual weakening until death.

At that time the survivors, who were to become known as *hibakusha,* explosion-affected people, did not know they were suffering from radiation effects. They only knew they had been contaminated in some terrible way.

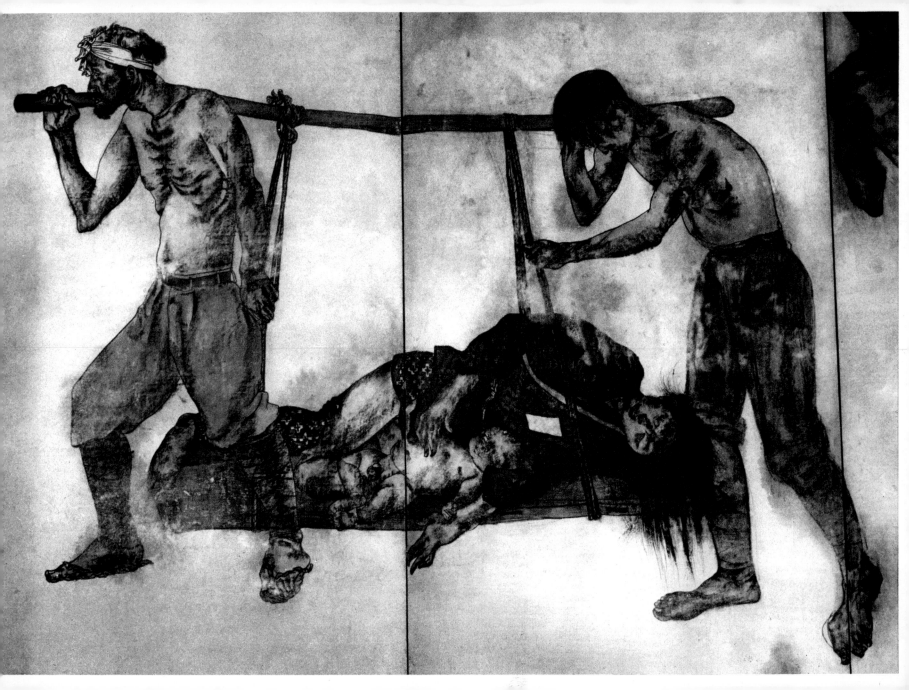

Within an instant the bomb destroyed sixty thousand houses in a three-mile radius. The flimsy wooden structures burned in the fury of the firewind that swept through them. Only the few buildings reinforced with concrete stood like spectres in the atomic wasteland.

There was the rumor that trees and flowers would never grow again in Hiroshima. That everyone who had been exposed to the bomb would be dead within three years. And that for seventy-five years no one could live there.

Trees and flowers are blooming again, as if Nature, herself, wants to forget this unnatural catastrophe.

And the Aioi Bridge, which was the target site of the Enola Gay, once more spans the Ohta River.

Perhaps, after all, you think, it is possible to forget.

But pass by the Sumitomo Bank.

The shadow of the man who sought refuge on its steps, still remains. He was imprinted there by the heat and light of the bomb's explosion, as if he were being photographed for posterity.

The steps have been left as a reminder—after a nuclear blast only the shadow of man remains, a shadow in the stone.

Visit the Atomic Dome in the Peace Park.

This ghostly structure has become the symbol of Hiroshima, linking the past and present in an uneasy alliance. Originally it was the Industrial Exhibition Hall, designed by an Austrian architect to display the perfectural wares. Now it displays the power of the first atomic bomb.

Over the years the dome was the center of bitter controversy. There were those who demanded it be torn down so that Hiroshima could forget its scars and become like any other city. Others insisted it should remain as a warning to the rest of the world. And a third group, with Asian resignation, suggested letting it stand until it fell naturally of its own force.

The local government finally resolved the issue. The Atomic Dome is to be preserved. Its wounded presence shall continue to preside over the city.

Stroll through the Peace Park.

In some ways it might be a park anywhere. People wander through it aimlessly, babies frolic on the grass, old men sit in the sun.

However, bus loads of children are brought in daily from all parts of the country on school tours. As if there is a lesson to be learned here.

You realize that the young, too, are foreigners in this place. Twenty-five years ago is a long time—long before they were born.

Pause at the Cenotaph.

This is the official Atomic Bomb monument. Within its graceful form are buried the names of those who perished. Even now as survivors die, their names are added to the sacred list.

You watch people come up and lay flowers or light incense. And standing there before the simple grandeur of this abstract structure, you are seized with a moment of piety, as if you were visiting an old church in Europe, or a ruin in Greece.

This hallowed ground where the souls of the dead are believed to reside draws you into its sorrow. For that moment you peer into the deep abyss created by an atomic explosion. And you, too, are a survivor.

Look at the Children's Monument.

Decorated with thousands of folded paper cranes, it is a memorial to all young people who suffered from the bomb. But it was not erected until 1958, after the death of Sadako Sasaki.

Sadako has been called the Anne Frank of Hiroshima. Her death from delayed radiation effects twelve years after the bomb fell, seemed to symbolize man's inhumanity to man more than all the statistics and scientific facts about the nature of nuclear weapons.

Sadako was only two at the time the *pikadon* exploded a mile from her home, and she seemed unharmed. She appeared to be a normal, healthy girl until she was in the sixth grade. Then she suddenly developed the signs of leukemia so well known among Hiroshima survivors.

According to the legend which has grown up around her, Sadako was very brave in the hospital. "I don't want to die," she wrote solemnly in her diary, yet she managed to laugh and sing gayly when her classmates came to visit her. And she folded paper cranes.

There is an old belief in Japan that a crane can live a thousand years. If you fold a thousand paper cranes, they will protect you from illness. But Sadako did not have the strength or time to reach a thousand. In October of 1955 when she had made only nine hundred sixty-four, she died. Her friends added the missing cranes and placed them all in the coffin with her.

And then, as if the young people of Hiroshima could no longer bear watching their friends die slowly over the years, they rose up together to do something about it. They would erect a monument to Sadako in the Peace Park to remind the grown-up world what the bomb had done to the first children who experienced it.

With the zeal of crusaders Sadako's classmates started a campaign to raise money from all over Japan. To the amazement of their impoverished elders in that struggling city, they collected the miraculous sum of seven million yen (twenty thousand dollars), and commissioned a distinguished sculptor in Tokyo to design their monument for them.

It is a powerful memorial. On the top of an oval granite pedestal, which symbolizes Mt. Horai, the fabled mountain of paradise, Sadako stands, holding a golden crane in her outstretched arms. Beneath her are colorful paper leis, each a thousand cranes, that people from all over the world have placed there as offerings.

At the base are the words: "This is our cry, this is our prayer: peace in the world."

29

Go to the Peace Museum.

Let the pitiful testimony of inanimate things—rock, metal, tile, stones, glass—twisted by the malevolent heat into grotesque shapes—tell you their own story of this man-made disaster.

Many of these objects were gathered right from the burning ruins by a geologist who understood the historical importance of their bizarre configurations. While others searched through the charred remains for pots, knives and any other household items they might sell for survival, he collected his weird assortment of melted stones, roof-tiles and crockery to study and preserve. He even collected shadows.

As a victim he hoped that someday his rucksacks of rubble would confront man with the cruelty he had inflicted on Nature. As a scientist, he hoped to expose the "essence" of the atomic bomb experience.

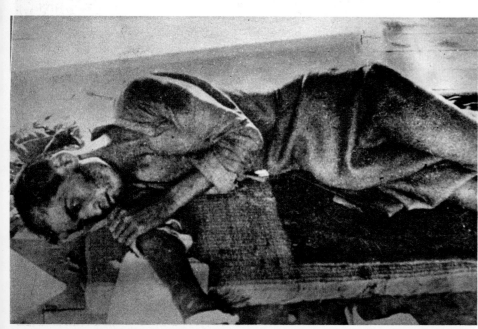

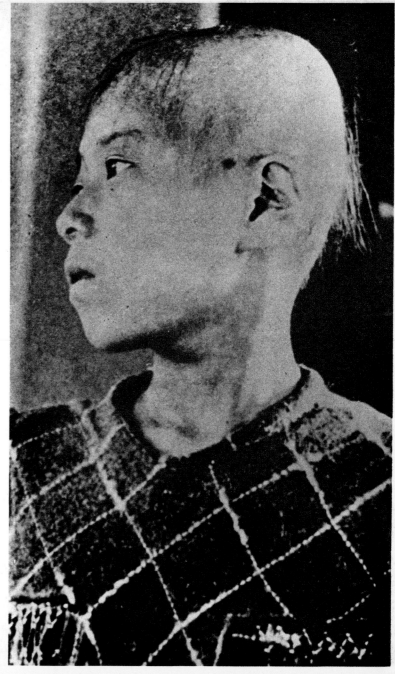

Walk through the museum.

You notice that adults hover nervously about photographs showing the city in ruins, the victims stretched out helplessly in barracks and warehouses.

They seem unable to believe that all this death and destruction could come about in a moment.

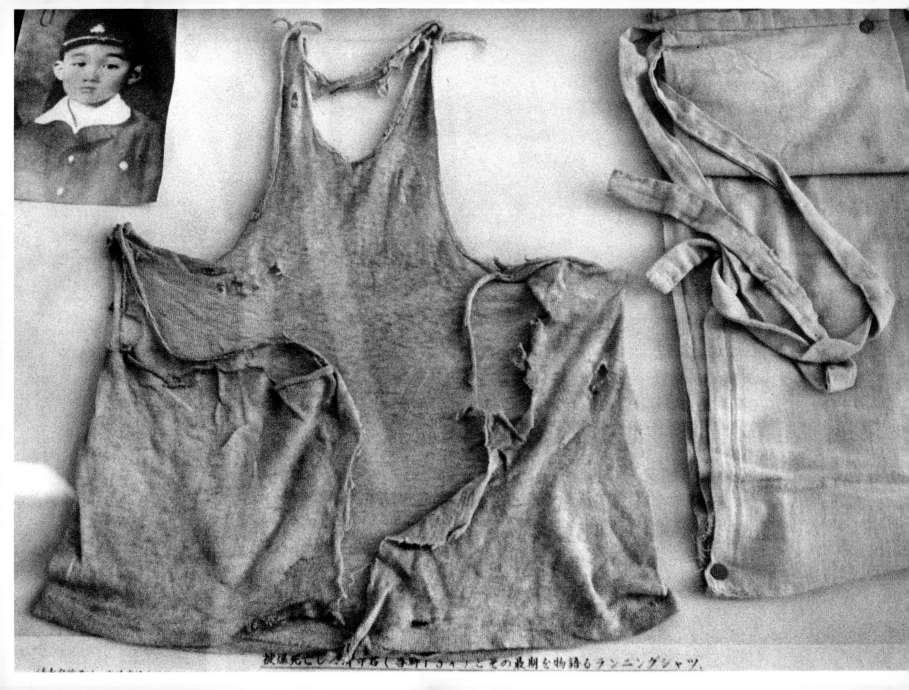

被爆死亡せし少年すする（享時十うハイとその最期を物語るランニングシャツ。

The young seem held by the uniform of a middle school boy that had turned to rags under the gamma rays of the bomb. He, like so many other students, was caught while tearing down houses in the center of the city to make fire lanes in case of attack.

Everyone is hushed going past the rows of life-size dummies modeling, as in some macabre fashion show, the tattered remnants of the garments worn that day.

One mannequin in particular attracts your attention. There is something so poignant about this maiden of sorrow as she stands there caught in that one terrible moment of time.

You feel compelled to trace the family of this woman, to know her story.

Her name was Ryoko Matsutani.

She was a gentle person who loved poetry, her husband tells you. She was thirty-three years old then, and her one regret was that she did not have children.

On that morning of August 6 she had been assigned to clear the fire lanes behind City Hall. She felt a strong flash, like a camera bulb going off in her face. When she regained consciousness sometime later, she groped along a railroad track, the one familiar path in the wilderness, to find her way home.

Ryoko's husband made a little tent for her in the back of the soy sauce factory that he managed. The skin hung from her swollen face, the upper part of her body was badly burned. They had only oil and flour to put on her wounds.

Her husband's mother came as fast as she could from Tokyo when she heard that Hiroshima had been annihilated. She hoped only to find the bones of her son and daughter-in-law to carry back to the ancestral grave. She could hardly believe they were alive.

But she came too late. Ryoko's hair was falling out, she had diarrhea and vomiting. When she saw her mother-in-

law, she wanted to be held like a baby. She died just three days later. Her last words were that she was sorry that she had not been able to have a child. She promised her husband that she would help him from the next world.

Ryoko's husband eventually remarried. When a daughter was born, his mother was convinced that the baby was the reincarnation of Ryoko.

Ryoko's mother-in-law was a strong woman, but she was overcome by the suffering she had seen in Hiroshima. She decided to purify herself by living for three years in a cave on the mountaintop of the holy island of Miyajima.

"I prayed for the soul of Ryoko, and that the baby born to my son should not suffer from the bomb," she says. "I prayed for the world, too. I hoped that when I returned to Hiroshima I would have special powers to help people."

Now she is a Shinto priestess, known to everyone as the *Yama-no-Obaasan,* the old woman of the mountain. Survivors come to the home that she shares with her son for talismen to take to the hospital or spiritual help to face their uncertain future.

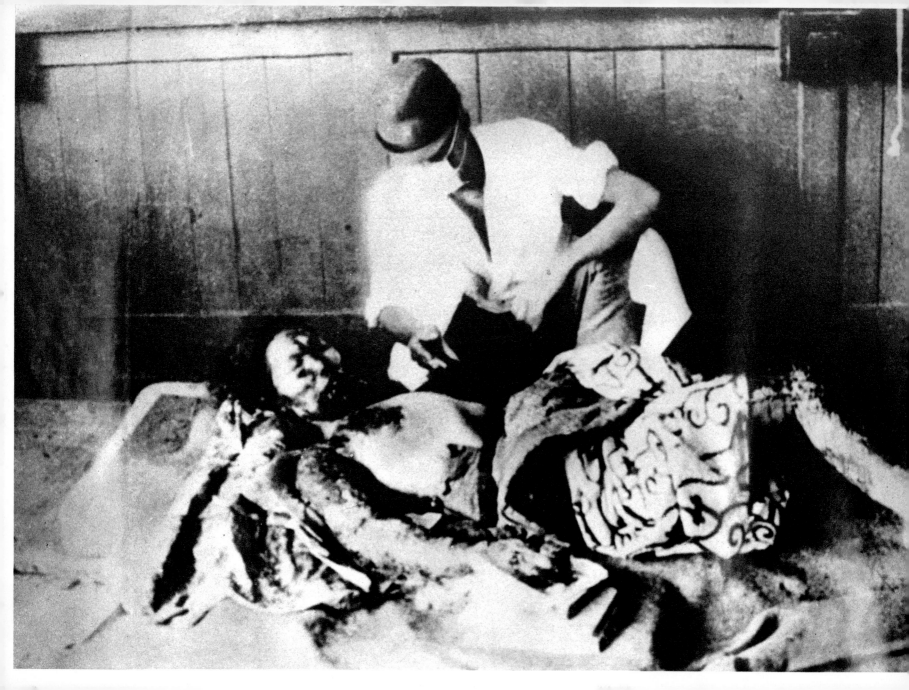

You learn that some of the badly wounded in the photographs did not die.

Recently a woman walked into the museum for the first time and recognized herself in a picture among the wounded at Danbara High School. She remembered the pattern of the kimono she had been wearing at the time. Now she is married and runs a gasoline station with her husband.

You go to visit this woman, Tsuyako Wataji.

She tells you that she usually does not talk about the bomb. She had only gone to the museum that day to please her daughter who wanted to see it.

"It was terrible to return to that time," she says. "I was twenty-two years old then and engaged to be married. I had volunteered to take my mother's place in the women's labor corps in the center of town. I remember even now dropping my lunch box off at my sister's house on the way, and looking at myself in the mirror as I left."

When she returned a short time later, her sister did not recognize her. Her face was black with ash, skin was hanging from her cheek, and rags from her body. They fled to the country house where the family had decided to meet in case of emergency.

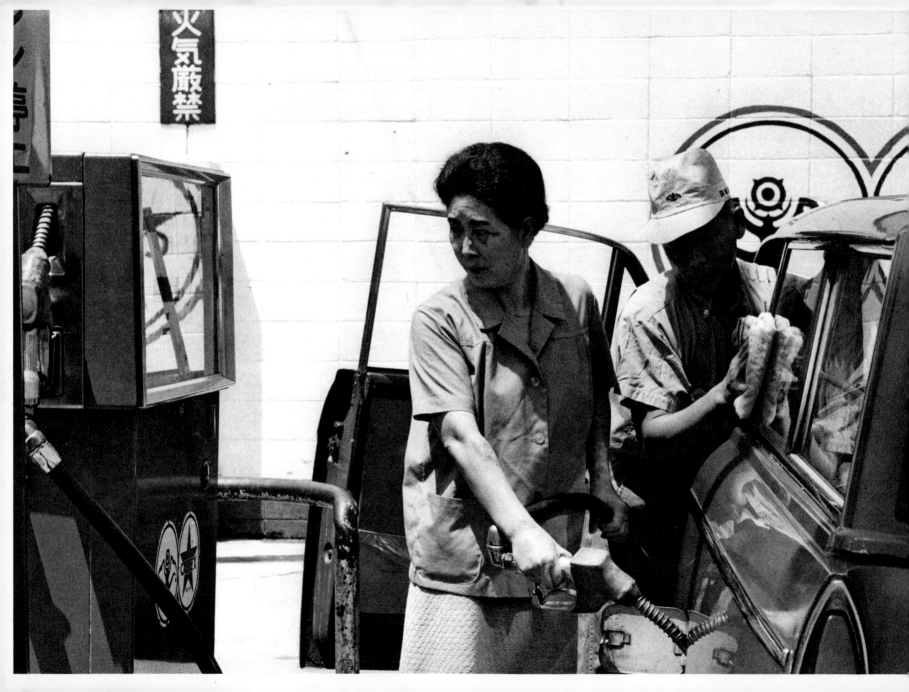

She found her mother already there. "If you can come this far, you can live," her mother told her. "I won't let you die from these burns."

When the army set up a dispensary at the Danbara High School, her family took her there on a stretcher. She could hear the flies buzzing over the charred bodies of the wounded in the fetid air of those hot August days. Many people had lost their families and had no one to attend them. They defecated or vomited right where they lay. One night she saw a soldier washing the maggots off a young girl. The next day that girl was dead.

"My mother and sister stayed with me all the time," she recalls. "They brought fresh grapes from the vineyard and sometimes milk and eggs. My mouth was so swollen I could hardly eat, but I drank a lot of tea. The army gave us honey."

She grew stronger in a few months, but her face was so disfigured few people could bear to look at her. When her fiancé got a job in Tokyo, she refused to marry him because she was ashamed to be seen by outsiders.

"A year later my childhood friend returned home from Southeast Asia where he had been a soldier. Because there was no love between us, I was not ashamed to see him. When we decided to marry, my mother was overjoyed. She used to tell me in those days, 'I don't care if you come home a day after marriage, but just let me see you in a bridal gown once!' "

They were farmers at first, but the work was too much for her. In the winter her hands would swell; in the summer her skin was too tender for sunlight. She opened the gasoline station to help support their three children.

Except for occasional fatigue she feels fine now. But dark reddish spots have recently appeared under her eyes. The doctor does not know what causes them.

"I just go on with my life day by day here at the gasoline station," she concludes. "I try not to worry that my children will come down with anything or that their children won't be normal. Compared to other survivors, I know I am lucky."

Now you understand that a city that has suffered from nuclear weapons is different from cities that were casualties of ordinary bombing.

And its people are different too. They harbor a deep fear of contamination within themselves; fear that they might at any moment come down with A-bomb disease.

What is A-bomb disease?

For the survivors, it is often any illness that afflicts them. For American and Japanese doctors, it is any disease that can be proven to be caused by radiation effects on the body. It takes years to get such proof, and there are still many questions left to be answered.

So far leukemia and cancer of the thyroid, cataracts and related eye conditions, are known to be specifically related to radiation.

There is increasing evidence that cancers of the stomach, lung, ovary and uterine cervix, several kinds of anemia, liver and blood disease have been caused by the bomb, as

44

well as endocrine and skin disorders, heart and kidney dis-
turbances, premature ageing, sexual dysfunctions and im-
pairment in the growth and development of exposed children.

Women who were four months or less pregnant at the
time of the bomb had stillbirths and abnormal babies,
which gave rise to the fear of producing monsters. No doctor can guarantee a mother that abnormalities will not
eventually appear in her children, her grandchildren and
even later generations.

What has been most difficult for doctors to evaluate is a
condition of general weakness and debilitation in the survivors. But whether or not this can be scientifically determined, it is clear that the victims feel they are carrying some
dark host of death within their bodies.

For the survivors, A-bomb disease has become as much
an emotional disease as a physical one. There is never an
end to anxiety.

Sometimes it seems to you that all roads in Hiroshima lead to the Atomic Bomb Hospital.

Completed in 1956, its one-hundred-twenty beds have become increasingly filled with the aged as the event moves farther and farther away. Free medical treatment was finally granted in 1957 to those who were within the city limits at the time of the holocaust, who came into the center of the city during the fourteen day period following it, who handled the dead or wounded, or who were in their mother's wombs.

Every admission causes a ripple below the surface of the survivor community. Every death creates a new wave of hysteria, as the local newspapers keep a faithful obituary list.

Dr. Fumio Shigeto, the head of the A-Bomb hospital, is a survivor himself.

Because of his warmth, as well as his position, he has become a kind of father figure to the *hibakusha* who came under his care. "It is getting difficult to tell who is suffering from A-bomb disease and who from the natural process of ageing," he says. "But I think it is both."

As for the young, there are always a few of them in the wards. And his office is usually filled with couples who come to him for advice on whether or not they should marry.

"I cannot say anything with certainty," he admits. "Last year a young woman married only a few months suddenly died of leukemia. And a young man with a wife and child, just as unexpectedly, became fatally ill. It makes everyone, even me, nervous when such things happen. I can only advise each couple that if they are doing well with their lives now, they might as well go ahead."

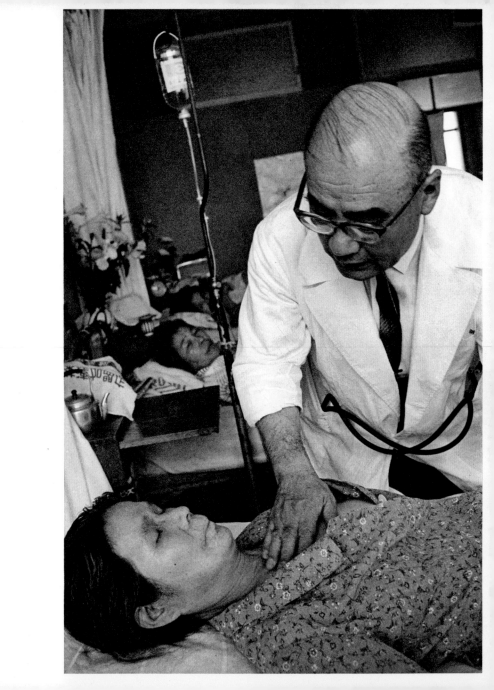

Not all the survivors who enter the A-Bomb hospital are terminal cases. Some like Shigeo Taguchi come in for minor treatment, like an elbow operation.

"I used to hate Americans," he says.

All of his family died from radiation effects a few months after the bomb fell. His eyesight was damaged, his arm useless. He drank continually and carried a knife, hoping to kill an American. It was a geisha who took the knife away from him. She told him he should plan his life, instead of hating others.

Now Mr. Taguchi is married and has three normal children. He is even the leader of a boy scout troop that is trying to exchange letters with an American troop. He has a job as clerk in a big rayon company.

"But don't get the idea my life is successful," he warns. "A survivor is always one step behind other people in promotion because he has to take so many medical leaves—like this one."

Mr. Taguchi wants to tell you a story—one he's always dreamed of telling an American about the day of the bomb.

"I was twenty-three years old then," he says, "and home on leave from the navy. There was a beautiful girl who lived next door, but I was too shy to talk to her. Her birthday was on August 6, and I was invited to the party.

"On that morning I woke early and went outside to see if I could catch a glimpse of her. Instead I saw something that looked like a pink ball falling through the sky. I thought some B-29 had dropped a flare by mistake. Suddenly it got dark. The next thing I knew I was pinned under the house.

"My father rescued me, and mother rounded up my sisters. As I fled through our garden, I saw the girl next door under a pillar of her fallen house. I ran to help her mother who was desperately trying to pull her out. We called to a group of soldiers running by, but they didn't hear us.

"The girl was conscious and begged her mother and me to escape as flames were whipping up all around us. We fled into the black rain that was pouring down over the city.

"I didn't come back to our house until a month later. I saw the girl next door burned to charred bones. Her mother was standing there in the ruins. She spoke to me about the birthday party we were all going to have together on August 6."

51

Mrs. Nishida, a farmer's wife, has been in the hospital for the past six years with severe anemia. She receives blood transfusions every few days.

She wasn't hurt when her boardinghouse, a mile from the center, collapsed. Since she was a nurse she spent the next month caring for the wounded in a hospital. She had to stop when she too became a patient with radiation symptoms.

"For the next seventeen years I was fine," she tells you. "Then suddenly I started getting dizzy and needing blood transfusions. I've been in and out of the hospital many times since then."

The hardest part is not being with her two children. Their farm is a two hour trip by bus, and they have so much schoolwork, they can't visit too often.

"I often think if women knew how terrible it is to be separated from their children, they would work hard for peace," she says.

Hiroshima is full of surprises—mostly unpleasant ones.

A reporter was assigned to do a feature on *Forgotten Hiroshima*. He probed around and found seventeen abnormal children in various parts of the city. They were all microcephalic, with small heads and mental retardation. Their mothers had been three or four months pregnant with them, and within two miles of the hypocenter.

Not only did the city not know about these children, the families did not know about each other. Most lived in depressed areas called *atomic slums*.

The children are now twenty-four years old. Their mental ages range from two to eleven. They are the size of a ten-year-old.

With the reporter's help, the families have organized The Mushroom Club. The title refers both to the mushroom shape of the cloud, and the fact that these children are growing like mushrooms in the shade.

The club wants government support; and it wants the world to know that nuclear weapons have given man the power to destroy his own species.

You go to visit Haruo Kamura.

His mother began to notice that he was slow to sit up during his first year. She was told it was due to insufficient diet.

At school, teachers believing he was suffering from normal retardation, allowed him to move ahead with his class until the sixth grade. At that time he could not read or write, but could recognize some characters in his name.

Haruo smiles at you cheerfully as you have tea with his mother. "He seldom gets angry," she says, "unless a child taunts him with names such as 'monkey'."

In the summer he plays ball outside with the four-and five-year-olds. In the winter he stays in bed, for he cannot bear the cold.

The Mushroom Club is asking the city to send Haruo to a home for the feeble minded in the nearby mountains. He is considered to be one of the most accomplished of the microcephalics. He shaves and is toilet trained.

56

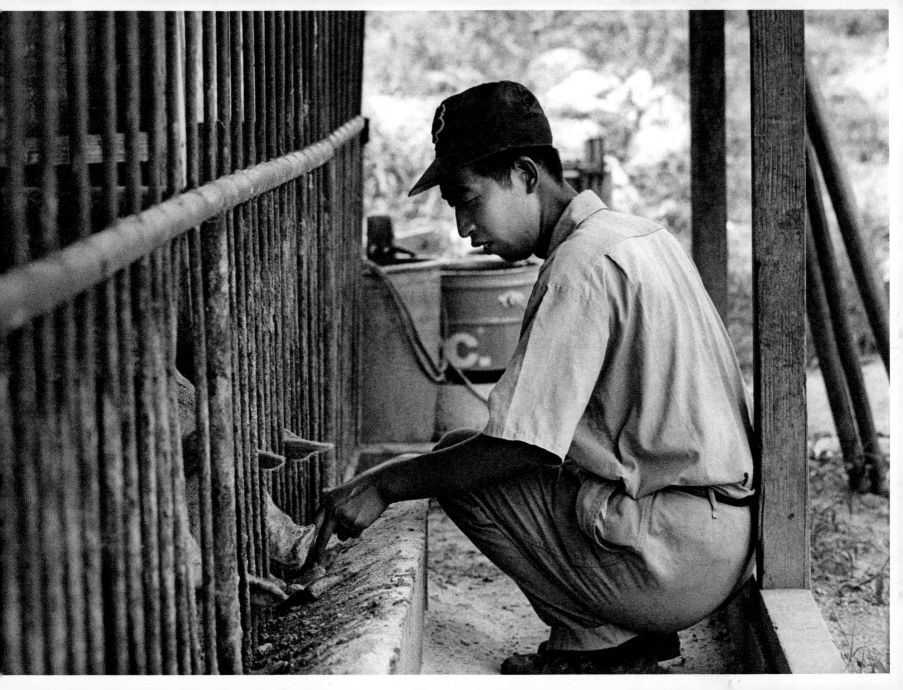

Yukiko Hatanaka is not toilet trained. She has never developed beyond the mentality of a two-year-old, understanding only the simplest things. She speaks in gutteral tones. And since she cannot handle chopsticks, she eats with her fingers.

Yukiko's father, a barber, has in past years sent appeals to the governments of both Japan and America to help children like his daughter who were deformed by the bomb. But up to now no one has shown an interest in their plight.

What about the children who had just been born when the bomb fell? The youngest are twenty-five years old now. They can remember nothing—but neither can they forget.

Watching Yuki Muneoka play with her kindergarten class, you cannot believe she has a care in the world. But you learn that she suffers from anemia and gets periodic blood transfusions.

Yuki believes that no one will marry her. "Japanese consider survivors tainted," she says. "They want women in the family who will produce healthy children."

Other people's children may be all Yuki will ever have in her uncertain life.

What became of the children who were orphaned on that August 6?

Many of them were raised just outside Hiroshima Harbor, on the island of Ninoshima, otherwise known as Boy's Island.

The orphanage was founded in the fall of 1946 when an idealist schoolteacher was troubled by the thousands of vagrants hanging around the railroad station, taking part in black marketeering and prostitution. He felt the island, away from the temptations of delinquent life, would be the best place for these homeless waifs.

One night he went out with a truck and literally abducted sixty orphans at the station. He took off at high speed for the pier. When he got there he had only forty-three boys left, but they were the original ones to come to Boy's Island.

The orphans have all grown up. There is only one left, Yoshiki Yamanouchi. He was ten years old when he arrived with scars over half of his body. His mother, a widow, was killed on her way to work in the building that is now the Atomic Dome.

Why does he stay when the others have all gone back to the mainland? He cannot quite say. He knows that he does not feel close to this new generation of children. They are not war orphans. They have never had the nightmares of those who have lived through an atomic blast.

Perhaps it is because he does not want to face the cruel realities outside. Japan is a family-centered society that discriminates against orphans, as well as survivors. Companies prefer employees with relatives who will be responsible for them.

Once a week Yoshiki takes the small island ferry to the mainland. He likes to listen to music, drink beer and play *pachinko,* the popular pinball machine. But he doesn't spend too much because he is saving for the day he will finally leave.

His dream—to have a piece of land where he can build his own house, and have a memorial stone for his family.

What of the young people who were born to survivors years after the bomb? Were they able to escape from its shadow?

You meet Yoko Kurokawa in a small coffee shop. She is an attractive nineteen-year-old who enjoys talking and laughing with the customers. But her smile is masking the grim reality that she is supporting two aged parents who are suffering from radiation effects.

Yoko takes you to the two straw-matted rooms over a milk shop that she and her family call home.

"I feel I am twenty-five years old, because twenty-five years have passed since the bomb fell," her father tells you. "I died at that moment. And when I recovered, a few months later, from acute radiation symptoms, I felt as if I was reborn."

Being reborn was not easy. From the ruins of his house, Mr. Kurokawa recovered only a sake bottle that had melted into a dish. Suffering from anemia, as well as kidney and heart trouble, he was in and out of the hospital. His wife, who was weak herself, was forced to take in sewing to pay the medical expenses.

Yoko's two older brothers left home immediately after junior high school. They wanted to start a new life away from Hiroshima and all the troubles they had seen there.

Her older sister is married and has a family of her own. Only Yoko is left to care for her parents.

Yoko leaves with you to return to the coffee shop. She meets her boyfriend there. She has not told him her family are *hibakusha*.

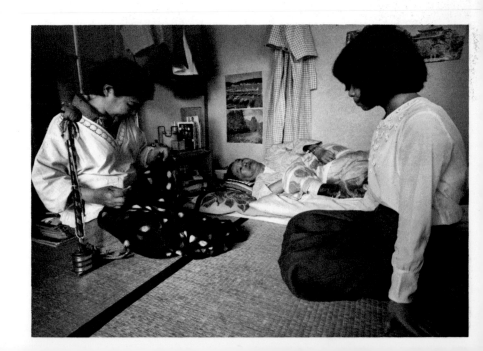

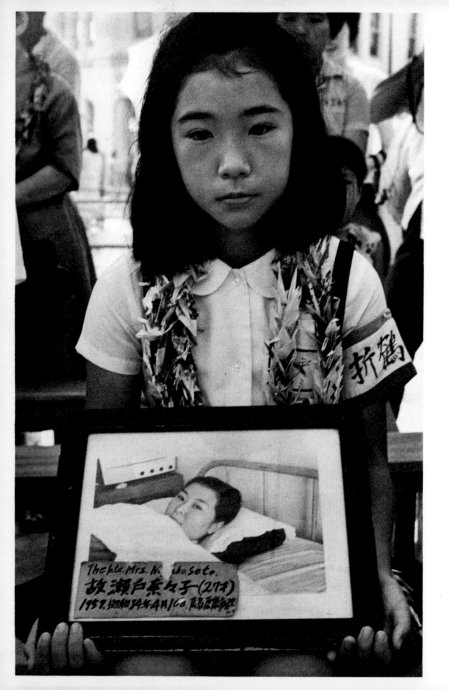

Mami-chan is only twelve now.

Her mother, Nanako Seto, died of leukemia caused by delayed radiation effects, when she was just a baby.

From the time she could walk, Mami-chan, accompanied by her grandmother, has carried her mother's deathbed picture in her arms, much as she has carried the pain in her heart, to anti-war parades, to August 6 ceremonies, to any commemoration that is held for *hibakusha*.

You can understand what holds Mami-chan to her mother when you read the diary she kept in the hospital. After her death it was entitled: *A Crane That Cannot Come Back*.

January 29, 1957

I cannot help but think of the future of Mami-chan. I want her to be a well-educated person—even if she is only a girl. I do not want her to have an experience like mine. Oh, how I wish I could hold her in my arms all the time. I am so afraid she will forget me since I do not see her often.

February 22, 1958 (on returning to the hospital from an overnight visit home).

My sweet home ˜ had not seen it for almost nine months. How difficult to return here. The chilliness of the corridor. Time to turn off lights soon—lonely. Tears stream down—ceaselessly. One more patient has died tonight. I don't want to die. Mami, my only daughter. Nanako, Mami's only mother! Oh, this feeling—this lonely feeling.

(This was her last entry. She died at 10:45 A.M. on April 10, 1959.)

Mami-chan was reared by her grandmother. A solitary child who seldom smiles, she is a crane who cannot forget.

There are survivors' children who are determined to forget.

Takaki Kubo is one. He is a salesman for a paste factory. Some of his nine brothers and sisters still carry the scars from shattered glass when the bomb fell two miles from their home. But he was in the shelter and uninjured.

"I never think about what happened here," he says. "When I am finished with work, I bowl, go to bars and the movies. I want to be the same as others."

But can he?

The next time you see him at his office he is more frank. He became aware of being a *hibakusha* when he worked in a distant town. People regarded him as something different when they learned he was from Hiroshima. They talked about radiation effects, how they would never marry a survivor.

Now he worries occasionally about the children he might have if he marries. But still he says he has no interest in peace activities. "I want to forget the whole thing, to have a good time."

The same is true for Yoshio Minagawa.

Only the scar on his right cheek suggests there are things about his life he is not telling you. He talks continually about mahjong, which he loves to play all night.

Yoshio lost his father, a brother and a sister, but he insists he has grown up in a normal way. "I know that some survivors have had a difficult time, but my life was not affected by the bomb."

Yet with him too, the denial begins to weaken as you get to know him better. He admits feeling a certain amount of anxiety about radiation effects, but it is only after his mother joins you that you learn the true situation.

"Yoshio gets overtired from the all-night mahjong games," she says. "He has nosebleeds and needs blood transfusions. And he cannot drink anything, for his body will not accept alcohol."

Yoshio's smile is both affectionate and nervous as his mother speaks. "She worries too much," he says. "That is why our generation does not like to talk about our fears. We consider them taboo. It is better to talk about ordinary things."

73

Everyone in Hiroshima faces this problem—how much to remember, how much to forget.

Hiromu Morishita is one of Hiroshima's many individuals who is determined that the world not forget.

At first glance you want to turn away from him. You are embarrassed, even guilty. The bomb seems to have seared into his very being, leaving huge, unsightly keloid scars. But then you are attracted by the inner beauty of this man, who is both a poet and calligrapher, as he tells you how he struggled for many years to find a significant way to live, how he finally came to realize that his only salvation was to work for peace in a personal way.

Mr. Morishita feels that the young people he teaches calligraphy to cannot understand his generation because they have not experienced the unexpected. Through his writings he is trying to convey the dangers of nuclear weapons to them.

"I shall keep working as long as nations are threatened by war," he says. "The hope of the world lies with the young people. They must realize the danger before it is too late."

The members of the *Orizurukai,* the Folded Crane Club, will not let the city forget.

The group was founded in 1958 by the boys and girls who raised money for Sadako Sasaki's monument. It has been kept going by the unswerving zeal of Ichiro Kawamoto and his wife, Tokie, both bomb survivors, who are determined that children shall never again suffer from the savagery of nuclear war.

Some men are meant to be the conscience of their time, to bear witness. Ichiro Kawamoto is one of them. Over the years he has taken only menial jobs so that he can have the necessary time to guide the club's activities: visiting survivors in the hospital; assisting the ill at home; holding memorial services for the children who have died; writing messages to heads of state and the United Nations protesting nuclear testing and pleading for universal disarmament.

The members, now mostly high school girls, are also in correspondence with the survivors of Auschwitz and send annual messages of condolence to the families of those who lost their lives at Pearl Harbor.

There are some in the community who accuse Kawamoto and his wife of running a cult of the dead.

Perhaps it is that—but for them, Hiroshima is a city of the dead. It can only be redeemed in a world in which nuclear weapons are no more.

Whatever the urge to forget, August 6 is each year's official reminder. On that day the City of Peace acts out its fate.

For weeks in advance municipal and private organizations make frenzied preparations. Labor unions and peace groups march through the streets to the Cenotaph. Political workers seem to get stronger, survivors weaker, as the day approaches.

For August 6 no longer belongs to the survivors alone.

It has been taken over as a day of protest as well as a day of commemoration. The annual meeting of the International Conference Against the A- and H-Bombs and the rival factions which have splintered off from it, draw participants from abroad.

Some survivors feel like the pawns of these bickering political groups. Others feel fulfilled by them. How else will their cry be heard?

Return to Hiroshima on August 6.

The city seems frozen in time. Once again the Enola Gay seems to cast its shadow over everything.

The survivors and their families have been gathering in the park since dawn.

At 8:15 A.M. everyone bows his head in prayer for one minute. There is a silence as strong as the blast must have been on that original day.

The mayor makes a plea for peace at the Cenotaph. Other dignitaries say a few words. Fresh flowers are offered the dead. White doves are released, like free spirits, into the sky.

After the main ceremony at the Cenotaph, the members of the Folded Crane Club hold a special one at the Children's Monument.

They bring black-ribboned pictures of the children who have died to share this moment with them.

And new paper cranes join the old.

That night there are fireworks and other festivities in the Peace Park, which seem strange to you. But they are related to the Buddhist custom of keeping the dead company, of easing their loneliness.

The members of the Folded Crane Club, oblivious to everything around them, walk with paper lanterns through the city and float them down the Ohta River to console the spirits of their departed friends.

Each lantern has a child's name. As they drift out to sea, the children sing a song by a poet of the people, and a friend of the young, the late Sankichi Toge:

> Give back my father, give back my mother,
> Give grandpa back, grandma back,
> Give our sons and daughters back.
>
> Give me back myself, give mankind back,
> Give each back to each other.
>
> So long as this life lasts,
> Give peace back to us,
> Peace that will never end.

And then the city sleeps.

DATE DUE